Contemplations Of A Reticent Soul

Dr Shebna Sithara

BookLeaf Publishing

India | USA | UK

Made with ❤ on the BookLeaf Publishing Platform
www.bookleafpub.in
www.bookleafpub.com

Dedication

Dedicated to my father who brought me the boon of
language

Preface

Contemplations of the reticent soul is a humble attempt to highlight the beauty of the world around us as well as within despite the chaos that exist. This collection of poems was derived in an effort to help realize the acceptability of a fair amount of imperfection in the quest for perfection. I hope my readers enjoy the lines feeling relaxed, yet give some deep thought about the complexity of human nature.

Acknowledgements

I express my deepest gratitude to my parents who gave me their best. I am ever grateful to my loving husband who enthusiastically supports my varying interests and constantly has to hold the fort down. Thankyou my lovely girls. You are the reason for my thorough introspection.

I greatly appreciate my publishers for giving me a chance to make a forever wish come true. Their constant motivation truly helped bear fruit.

Mystic trails

At the crack of dawn
As I set out to stroll
The crisp cool morning air
Gently fills my soul.

Though scarcely visible
The way ahead
Through the mist
I gaily tread.

Aside the river
With its virtuous gurgle
Nature's symphony
Matching the burble

Calls of the hornbills
Whispers of the breeze
Chatter of the babblers
Heart set at ease.

Twisting and turning
As the path grew
Soft light gently fills up
Gifting scenes anew.

Bustling magpie-robins
Fanning black and white tails
A peacock strut close by
Showing its fine details.

Spiders resting on cobwebs
Weighed down with a shimmer
A pair of coucals hopping busy
Bathing in the morning glimmer

On my way back home
Basking in the golden glaze
Even a thousand such mornings
Will never cease to amaze

With the flow

Rays of sunshine peering through the foliage
Rouse me from my sound sleep
Wide awake, I embark on a journey
Oblivious where the path would lead
Through the depths of the dense jungle
Toying with toppled tree trunks
Over the magnificent pebbles
I swiftly and gently glide
Suddenly out of nowhere
I stumble upon an enormous rock
And as if that would stop me
Little by the rules do I abide
Cheerily from atop I leap off
And land with a graceful pose
I then rush along the meadows
Sashaying down the course
The rains feed me like a baby
Sometimes a bit too little
Sometimes a bit more
I flourish and nourish
The way I progress
Untill I have had enough
Thereupon its time to rest
Facing the limitless horizon

Into the eternal tranquil
Into the vastness I go

Hope

Daylight ditched the skies
And the heavens mourned
The demented waters full on vicious
Rabid waves rammed the hull
Floors strewn with empty cans
Cases of shattered porcelain once dear
Dusty leather boots, silk and cashmere
Depleted water cans rolling relentless
Fluttering airborne the little hammock
With the companion, now all alone
There lay a befuddled beating heart
Parched lips that dream of dampness
Sunken eyes stare into oblivion
Life as such; a curse or a boon

Dawn

Dewdrops falling off leaf tips
The little birdie couldn't catch it all
Another puddle on the ground

Looking back

Empty chairs
Scary mirrors
Hollow stares
Broken promises

Bumpy roads
Failing stitches
Cracking voices
Uncaptured pictures

Lost memories
Restless hearts
Treacherous thoughts
Searching eyes

Blooming flowers
Beaming faces
Joyous bundles
Warm embraces

Looks that soothe
Words that mend
Deeds that console
Faith that holds

The diet poem

Afresh into the kitchen
After a bustling day
As hungry as a bear
Sure to not overindulge
A light tea perhaps
Would certainly do no harm
As the water popped bubbles
The tea leaves twirled
It entered the cup solo
Ah! Needless desolation
In jumped the sugarcubes
With dairy held tight
Bread loaves on the counter
Eager to join the party
The refrigerator chilled along
Company isn't bad
No, peanut butter isn't butter
The spread grinned wide
A tired shrivelled lettuce
Groaned from somewhere
The plump and juicy sausages
Summoned the frying pan
What an inviting state of affairs!

Could anyone turn away from there

Weary

The clothes were hanged
The dishes were done
The floors were clean
By then the house was asleep
Still loads of chores to deal
As the night stood still
Her mind in a tussle
Emotions ran deep
Unheard and unseen
Not by the ailing feet
Nor by the failing beats
Desparation quite loud
As quiet as a mouse
She disappeared into darkness

The beginning

The blue misty mountains
The frosty fresh air
The winding steep narrow roads
The invigorating smell of pine trees
The breathtaking valley views
The lush green lawns and clovers
The shapely carved hedges
The swings that let you see the world
The roundabout that started the spins of life
The hallways with kid height black boards
The wooden planked noisy floor boards
The cute little named dorm rooms
The warm hearted souls that tended
The furry friends that plays along
The lessons food for the soul
The first memory that began it all

If the remains could talk

Body on the table to some may cause dismay
Was lively and thriving the other day
You'll never hear the tales they have to say

Skin may be not as fair as yours today
Once was nourished by the costliest clay
At the moment dark and shrivelled they lay

None will learn of their glorious display
With the kith and kin days spent gay
Nor of their tactics that went astray

Message to the future their choices relay
Collectively let's thankfully pray
And pass on the good someday

The witch

Away from the crowds
At the foot of the mountain
Lived a woman all alone
A woman who laughed
A woman who sparked
The talks of the town
She took no mates
She birthed no kids
Grew all her staples
And built own things
Had long black hair
Was tall and fair
Dressed just for her own
Smirked when they taunt her
Fought if they attacked her
'A witch she is' they declared

Trapped

Trapped like the fallen second hand of the clock
I can watch all around
Merely sit back pointlessly

Trapped like a kite flying in the sky
I feel the gusty wind
Yet tethers me mockingly

Trapped like a lagoon from the sea
I can see you from afar
Never near you can be

Trapped like a bullet in the gun
Its dark in here
But once out it'll cost you dear

Quiet

I need to sit alone
Then I miss them all at once
Hence chaos sure is inevitable

Glee

Sunshine peeps in between the curtains
Nestling into the cozy chair by open windows
With a warm mug of fragrant coffee
The monstera has grown a new hole in her leaf
Pink flowers bloomed among the white water lilies
My feline friend rubbing against my legs
Hooks tangling colorful yarn quite uniform
Blissful day for the heart and soul

What's for dinner ?

What's for dinner dear
Asked the mate
Fresh rice and chicken
Smile on his face
Groan from the other side
Pizza or noodles
The little one cried
Wouldn't fill the tummy
It was declared
Ensued the tantrums
This could end up bad
Negotiation strategies
Wracking the brain
Rice pizza with chicken it is
With a drive for dessert
Now its all fair

Walk with me

Walk with me dear
Take me along under the cloudy skies
Through your valleys of pain
Over the hills of despair
On the roads of your troubles
Together let's cross rivers of woe

And when at nightfall
The hyenas growl
Your fears grow larger
Hold me strong
I'll be your light, forever delight
Dire straits will sure draw to a close

Trees

Swaying in the gentle breeze
After eternity of watching the sky roll
One day just a stump

Hideout

Rush along and hide
Where you can be lost in sight
Maybe lets do so outside
In the garden thickets
But thats where bees come by
Up on the tree
But the branch may give way
Beside the garage wall
But snakes may be the company
Or perhaps lets head inside
Behind the heavy curtains
But thats where spiders wait
Inside the laundry basket
But the stink might put me off
Under the giant bed
But the dust will cost me sure
Countless places to hide
But none perfect today

Half my child

Half my child
Please don't cry
You are confused
I wouldn't deny

Half my child
Don't feel dejected
Sorry for your desolation
You would be wondering why

Half my child
How to make up to you
The bundles of gifts
In fact doesnt seem to ply

Half my child
Words fall short of consolation
Your weeks are split up
Wish time would rush by

Half my child
Let me hold you tight
Forgive me for the dearth I've created
Be strong and live head held up high

Beach upon the mountain

Lost in corridors that leads nowhere
Winding stairways ending bizzare
Terrifying moments strip you bare
Stuck in an ever-repeating nightmare

All of a sudden the world is brand new
Gorgeous sunset with the waters blue
A shoulder for the head to rest on too
Beach upon the mountain, what a view!

Never enough

The lass is a little plumpy
She looks kind of dusky
Oh, she should have dieted
Got her skin bit brightened

The guy has gone bald
Developed a pot belly
Should have got his looks fixed
Workouts would have done him better

The baby is rather ugly
Who does she take after?
Tiny eyes from her fathers
Probably her mothers nose

Some souls just ever realise
How the harsh words agonize
Crush you without paying the price
Never enough will you be

Contemplations of a reticent soul

Lost among the noisy crowd
Eager to lay bare inside out
Echoing what goes around
Acknowledging the superficial charm

Would one again know of joy
That comes from looking eye to eye
When one's own thoughts let fly
Unmanipulated, gut felt and wise